Happy Baking!
Love, Linda
Andrea & Alyssa

MUFFINS

THE A TO Z COOKBOOK SERIES

Bar Cookies A to Z by Marie Simmons
Muffins A to Z by Marie Simmons

MUFFINS

Marie Simmons

Photography by Becky Luigart-Stayner
Calligraphy by Richard High

A Chapters Book

HOUGHTON MIFFLIN COMPANY
BOSTON   NEW YORK

Library of Congress Cataloging-in-Publication Data
Simmons, Marie.
Muffins A to Z / Marie Simmons; photographs by Becky Luigart-Stayner;
calligraphy by Richard High.
     p.   cm. — (The A to Z cookbook series)
Includes index.
ISBN 1-881527-91-3 (hardcover)
1. Muffins   I. Title.   II. Series.
TX770.M83S56 1995
641.8'15—dc20   95-14459

Produced in Italy by Sfera

Designed by Susan McClellan

Cover photograph: Blueberry Quickie-Mix Muffin, Strawberry Muffin,
Toasted Almond & Apricot Muffin, Devil's Food Chocolate Chip Muffin
Photograph by Becky Luigart-Stayner
Food styling by Marie Piraino

SFE 10 9 8 7 6 5 4 3

For Seraphina

Acknowledgments

As always, I am grateful for the care and guidance
I continue to receive from my editor, Rux Martin, and my agent, Judith Weber.
I am especially grateful to Susan Sarao Westmoreland for her excellent work and delicious
contributions, to Gretchen Semuskie for conscientiously retesting the recipes for me,
and to Susan McClellan for the warmth, sensitivity and style
she has given to the design of my A to Z books.

O *is for*
Oatmeal & Cranberry Muffins   58

P *is for*
Peanut Peanut-Butter Muffins   60
Pumpkin Praline Muffins   62
Prune & Oat Muffins with Orange   64

Q *is for*
Quickie-Mix Muffins   65

R *is for*
Raisin Bran Muffins   68
Ricotta-Lemon Muffins   70

S *is for*
Strawberry Muffins   71
Savory Scallion Muffins   73
Streusel Coffee Cake Muffins   74
Sweet Potato & Sugared Pecan Muffins   76

T *is for*
Toasted Almond & Apricot Muffins   78

Introduction

WHEN I WAS A TEENAGER, I loved working the Saturday morning breakfast shift at my uncle's diner. Sleek chrome, sparkling glass and shiny red Naugahyde, Joe's was the quintessential 1950s diner and a popular place for great home-cooked food.

As I frantically worked the counter, pouring coffee and serving the customers, the breakfast hour would peak. Then the rush would subside, and the tall pyramid of muffins I had carefully arranged before dawn would be reduced to ruins. By mid-morning, much to my relief, I would have a chance to retreat to a swivel stool at the end of the now empty counter, sip some hot tea and sink my teeth into a muffin, if there was one left.

The menu at Joe's boasted just two flavors of muffins: corn and bran. I ate the corn muffins toasted and slathered with creamy half-melted butter, enjoying the slightly gritty texture of the cornmeal between my teeth and the crunch of the toasted edges. The bran muffins I liked best at room temperature. Dark, dense and chewy, with big, plump raisins throughout, they were — and still are — my favorite muffin.

As I grew older and began baking for fun (and for a living), I moved on to making blueberry muffins, especially during the height of the summer season. With my repertoire of just three muffins —

corn, bran and blueberry—I was astonished when the muffin revolution took hold a few years back.

Suddenly, the muffin menu in coffee shops looked like the list of flavors in an ice cream parlor. Obviously the work of creative bakers determined to express themselves, the muffin business had advanced light-years beyond my conservative threesome. New flavors became routine: strawberry muffins, orange muffins, chocolate muffins, grated coconut and carrot muffins, even muffins made with, of all things, chocolate chips and M&M candies. As if to emphasize that this was a food trend to be reckoned with, many of these new muffins had grown from normal size to the diameter of a softball, often acquiring a texture to match.

As I began to experiment, I was determined to strike a balance between Joe's sensible but delicious muffins and the best of the new breed. I pledged that taste and texture, not size and off-beat ingredients, would be my criteria for a good muffin. I soon discovered that despite all the hype, muffins are not a complex food. They require few ingredients and not much in the way of equipment. Because they are quick to mix and even quicker to bake, they offer instant gratification. They can be dense and moist, light and airy, sweet or savory.

A big part of the fun is that muffins lend themselves to so many delicious interpretations. They can be cakelike or breadlike. They satisfy. They are easy to eat. And once a few simple techniques are mastered, they are not at all hard to make.

First, the dry ingredients are combined in one bowl and the liquid ingredients in another. The liquid ingredients are then added to the dry, all at once, and finally, everything is folded together gently, just until the batter is evenly moistened. Lumps are acceptable, even good: smoothness means that the batter has been overmixed, producing a tough muffin. In fact, the gummy texture of many store-bought muffins is caused by large commercial mixers, which overwork the batter.

Not surprisingly, many of my favorite muffin recipes are simply variations on the two basics that I first tasted while working the counter at Joe's. Applesauce Bran Muffins have joined my rendition of the classic bran and molasses with raisins. Plain cornmeal has been superseded by a slew of more sophisticated creations, including one made with both dried and fresh cranberries, another made with a combination of cornmeal and blueberry, whose taste is intensified by the addition of corn kernels, and a zippy cornmeal muffin with jalapeño peppers.

My muffin making isn't without whimsy. Devil's Food Chocolate Chip Muffins, Espresso Chip Muffins and Banana-Pecan Chocolate Chip Muffins (Knock-Out Muffins) have their place in this collection. And for those who want fresh-baked muffins but hate the idea of dragging out all the ingredients every time, I have devised a quick mix that can be made up ahead and stored in a canister, so a batch of banana, date-nut or blueberry muffins can be ready in just a few minutes.

Overall, my experience has taught me that a cool head when adding ingredients and a light hand when mixing are the sure ways to master the art of making muffins.

Muffin Mastery

1. Always preheat the oven. Most muffins are baked in a hot oven—400 degrees F—for a short period of time, about 20 to 25 minutes.

2. To ensure even baking, I use heavyweight muffin pans that have an easy-to-clean nonstick finish. My favorite pans are Ekco Baker's Secret. They are inexpensive, available everywhere from supermarkets to specialty shops and can be washed in the dishwasher.

3. Even if the muffin pans are nonstick, I usually coat them lightly with a nonstick cooking spray. If you prefer butter, melt it first and spread it lightly over the cups with a brush. Alternatively, paper or foil cupcake liners can be used.

4. Always measure flour by spooning it lightly into a dry metal or plastic measuring cup and then leveling off the top with a knife or flat spatula. Never dip the cup into the flour bin and never use a glass or liquid measure for flour, or the amounts will be significantly altered.

5. Sift baking soda through a small sieve when adding it to the dry ingredients. Instead of sifting together all the dry ingredients, I usually just stir them thoroughly. However, baking soda can have small stubborn lumps that won't dissolve even when the muffin is baked, and there is nothing more unpleasant than the soapy taste of a lump of baking soda. To solve this problem, I measure the baking soda into a small fine-mesh strainer that has been set over the bowl of dry ingredients and then sift it right into the bowl, rubbing out any small lumps of soda with the back of the measuring spoon.

6. After the dry ingredients have been combined in a large bowl, measure the liquid ingredients into a separate bowl. Once the ingredients are assembled, it takes less than a minute to mix up a batch of muffins. A whisk is the fastest, most effective tool for thoroughly incorporating the egg and other ingredients. Pour the liquid ingredients all at once over the dry ingredients and quickly fold them together with a large rubber spatula just until the batter is evenly moistened. The batter should be lumpy. Do not overmix. Don't be tempted to beat the batter, or your muffins will be tough and rubbery.

7. Master the art of folding. Slowly pull the spatula along the side of half of the bowl, then change direction and pull the spatula halfway across the bottom of the bowl and up through the center of the batter. Turn the bowl and repeat the process three or four more times until the batter is evenly moistened.

8. The recipes in this collection all make 12 muffins, in muffin cups that are about 3 inches in diameter. Depending on the quantity of batter, some of the muffins will be large and some will be medium-sized. I use a large kitchen tablespoon to distribute the muffin batter evenly among the muffin cups. Some people prefer to use a ¼-cup measure, others use a spring-driven ice cream scoop. The important thing is to distribute the batter evenly so that the muffins will be fairly uniform in size and bake at the same rate.

9. Because muffins can be ready quickly, they are perfect for serving fresh from the oven. They are best that way, or split and reheated in a toaster oven. Leftover muffins can be wrapped in foil and reheated in a 350-degree oven for about 10 minutes.

10. Leftover muffins also freeze very well. I like to use clear resealable freezer bags.

Almond Crumb Cake Muffins

T HE COMBINATION OF CHOPPED ALMONDS AND BUTTERY CRUMBS makes these tender muffins irresistible.

Topping

⅓	cup chopped natural (unblanched) almonds
¼	cup packed light brown sugar
¼	cup unbleached all-purpose flour
2	tablespoons (¼ stick) unsalted butter, melted

Batter

2½	cups unbleached all-purpose flour
½	cup sugar
2	teaspoons baking powder
1	teaspoon baking soda, sieved
½	teaspoon salt
1½	cups buttermilk
6	tablespoons (¾ stick) unsalted butter, melted
2	large eggs
¼	teaspoon almond extract

1. Preheat the oven to 400 degrees F. Lightly butter 12 muffin cups or coat with nonstick cooking spray.

2. **To make the Topping**: In a small bowl, combine the almonds, brown sugar and flour. Stir in the melted butter; set aside.

3. **To make the Batter**: Combine the flour, sugar, baking powder, baking soda and salt in a large bowl; stir until well blended. In a separate bowl, whisk together the buttermilk, melted butter, eggs and almond extract. Add to the dry ingredients all at once and fold just until evenly moistened. Do not overmix.

4. Divide the batter evenly among the muffin cups. Press 1 tablespoon of the topping onto each muffin.

5. Bake until the tops are golden and a toothpick inserted in the centers comes out clean, 22 to 25 minutes. Cool on a wire rack before removing from the pan.

MAKES 12 LARGE MUFFINS

Altamont Orchards Apple-Oatmeal Muffins

THESE LIGHT, TENDER MUFFINS remind me of my childhood breakfast of oatmeal sprinkled with cinnamon and sweetened with a stream of maple syrup. I added chopped apple and named them for Altamont Orchards, where every October, I conduct cooking demonstrations and cookbook signings at an apple festival near Albany, New York.

2 cups unbleached all-purpose flour	1 cup peeled, cored, chopped apple (1 large apple)
1 cup quick (not instant) oatmeal	1 cup buttermilk
2 teaspoons ground cinnamon	1 cup vegetable oil
2 teaspoons baking powder	½ cup maple syrup
½ teaspoon baking soda, sieved	½ cup packed light brown sugar
½ teaspoon salt	1 large egg

1. Preheat the oven to 400 degrees F. Lightly butter 12 muffin cups or coat with nonstick cooking spray.

2. Combine the flour, oatmeal, cinnamon, baking powder, baking soda and salt in a large bowl; stir until well blended. Add the apple; toss to coat.

3. In a separate bowl, whisk together the buttermilk, oil, maple syrup, brown sugar and egg. Add to the dry ingredients and fold just until evenly moistened. Do not overmix.

4. Divide the batter evenly among the muffin cups. Bake until the tops are golden and a toothpick inserted in the centers comes out clean, 20 to 22 minutes.

5. Cool on a wire rack before removing from the pan.

MAKES 12 LARGE MUFFINS

Applesauce Bran Muffins

BRAN MUFFINS ARE A FAVORITE OF MINE, and I am always looking for a recipe that is rich, nutty, moist and not overly dense. This one fits the bill. The applesauce adds a nice tang as well as extra moistness.

2 cups bran cereal (All-Bran or 100% Bran)
¾ cup milk
½ cup unsweetened applesauce
½ cup unsulphured dark molasses
⅓ cup vegetable oil
2 large eggs
1½ cups unbleached all-purpose flour

2 teaspoons baking powder
1 teaspoon baking soda, sieved
½ teaspoon salt
1 cup raisins
1 cup chopped, peeled, cored apple (1 large apple)

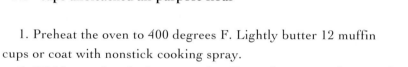

1. Preheat the oven to 400 degrees F. Lightly butter 12 muffin cups or coat with nonstick cooking spray.

2. Whisk together the bran cereal, milk, applesauce, molasses, oil and eggs in a medium bowl until blended. Let stand for 5 minutes.

3. In a large bowl, combine the flour, baking powder, baking soda and salt; stir until well blended. Add the raisins and apple; toss to coat.

4. Add the bran mixture to the dry ingredients; fold just until evenly moistened. Do not overmix.

5. Divide the batter evenly among the muffin cups. Bake until a toothpick inserted in the centers comes out clean, 20 to 22 minutes. Cool on a wire rack before removing from the pan.

MAKES 12 MEDIUM MUFFINS

Bacon Double-Corn Muffins

THESE TENDER, CREAMY AND DELICIOUS SAVORY MUFFINS are great for breakfast or for lunch or supper, served with soup and a salad. They are even good without the bacon.

4   strips lean bacon

1½ cups unbleached all-purpose flour

1   cup yellow cornmeal

¼   cup sugar

2   teaspoons baking powder

½   teaspoon baking soda, sieved

1   teaspoon salt

1   cup buttermilk

½   cup canned creamed corn
    (from one 14-ounce can)

⅓   cup vegetable oil

1   large egg

1. Preheat the oven to 400 degrees F. Lightly butter 12 muffin cups or coat with nonstick cooking spray.

2. Cook the bacon in a skillet until crisp. Drain on a paper towel; cool. Cut into ¼-inch pieces; set aside.

3. Combine the flour, cornmeal, sugar, baking powder, baking soda and salt in a large bowl; stir until well blended. Add the bacon. In a separate bowl, whisk together the buttermilk, corn, oil and egg until blended. Add the liquid ingredients to the dry all at once and fold just until evenly moistened. Do not overmix.

4. Divide the batter evenly among the muffin cups. Bake until the tops are golden and a toothpick inserted in the centers comes out clean, 20 to 25 minutes. Cool on a wire rack before removing from the pan.

MAKES 12 MEDIUM MUFFINS

Blueberry Corn Muffins

THIS FAVORITE RECIPE IS ADAPTED FROM FRIEND, cookbook author and fellow *Bon Appétit* columnist Richard Sax. I have added a tiny bit more sugar and a half-cup of corn kernels to reinforce the flavor. These are so moist and good that I used them to bribe the landlord of an apartment building I wanted to move into. I got the apartment.

1½   cups unbleached all-purpose flour
½   cup yellow cornmeal
½   cup sugar
1   tablespoon baking powder
1   teaspoon baking soda, sieved
¼   teaspoon salt
1½   cups (about ½ pint) fresh blueberries, rinsed, sorted and patted dry

½   cup fresh corn (cut from 1 ear), or thawed frozen or drained canned corn kernels
1   cup buttermilk
3   large eggs
¼   cup (½ stick) unsalted butter, melted

1. Preheat the oven to 400 degrees F. Lightly butter 12 muffin cups or coat with nonstick cooking spray.

2. In a large bowl, combine the flour, cornmeal, sugar, baking powder, baking soda and salt; stir until well blended. Add the blueberries and corn kernels; toss to coat.

3. In a separate bowl, whisk together the buttermilk, eggs and melted butter until smooth. Add to the dry ingredients all at once and fold just until evenly moistened. Do not overmix.

4. Divide the batter evenly among the muffin cups. Bake until the tops are golden and a toothpick inserted in the centers comes out clean, 20 to 25 minutes.

5. Cool on a wire rack before removing from the pan.

MAKES 12 MEDIUM MUFFINS

Christmas Muffins

O N CHRISTMAS MORNING, after all the packages were opened and the torn paper and ribbons cleared away, I decided to make a batch of hot muffins, whose red and green colors make them appropriately festive. Every cakey bite delivers the pleasant contrast of the concentrated sweetness of the dried berries and the refreshing bite of fresh ones. Dried cranberries, once a rarity, are now in my supermarket year-round. If they are unavailable in your market, you can substitute raisins. These muffins are great with a steaming mug of spiced cider.

½	cup fresh or frozen cranberries	½	cup dried cranberries
2	cups unbleached all-purpose flour	¾	cup plain low-fat yogurt
⅔	cup sugar	½	cup (1 stick) unsalted butter, melted
1	tablespoon baking powder		
½	teaspoon baking soda, sieved	½	cup milk
1	teaspoon ground cinnamon	1	large egg
½	teaspoon salt	½	cup chopped unsalted pistachios

1. Preheat the oven to 400 degrees F. Lightly butter 12 muffin cups or coat with nonstick cooking spray.

2. Coarsely chop the fresh cranberries in a food processor; set aside.

3. In a large bowl, combine the flour, sugar, baking powder, baking soda, cinnamon and salt; stir until well blended. Stir the fresh and dried cranberries into the dry ingredients.

4. In a separate bowl, whisk together the yogurt, melted butter, milk and egg until smooth. Add to the dry ingredients all at once and fold just until evenly moistened. Do not overmix.

5. Divide the batter evenly among the muffin cups. Sprinkle the pistachios evenly on the tops. Bake until the tops are golden and a toothpick inserted in the centers comes out clean, 20 to 22 minutes.

6. Cool on a wire rack before removing from the pan.

MAKES 12 MEDIUM MUFFINS

Cinnamon-Ripple Coffee Cake Muffins

THE BEST COFFEE CAKE IN A MUFFIN CUP you will ever experience. The cake part is simply an adaptation of a classic light buttermilk batter, with a sweet, buttery brown-sugar-and-cinnamon crumb mixture that is swirled in before baking.

Cinnamon Ripple

- ½ cup packed light brown sugar
- ¼ cup (½ stick) unsalted butter, softened
- ¼ cup unbleached all-purpose flour
- 2 teaspoons ground cinnamon

Batter

- 2½ cups unbleached all-purpose flour
- ½ cup sugar
- 2 teaspoons baking powder
- 1 teaspoon baking soda, sieved
- ½ teaspoon salt
- 1¼ cups buttermilk
- ½ cup (1 stick) unsalted butter, melted
- 2 large eggs
- 1 teaspoon vanilla extract

1. Preheat the oven to 400 degrees F. Lightly butter 12 muffin cups or coat with nonstick cooking spray.

2. **To make the Cinnamon Ripple:** Combine the brown sugar, butter, flour and cinnamon in a small bowl. Work together with a fork or your fingertips until well blended; set aside.

3. **To make the Batter:** Combine the flour, sugar, baking powder, baking soda and salt in a large bowl; stir until well blended. In a separate bowl, whisk together the buttermilk,

melted butter, eggs and vanilla until smooth. Add the liquid ingredients to the dry ingredients all at once and fold just until moistened. Sprinkle with the Cinnamon Ripple and fold once or twice to distribute evenly. Do not overmix.

4. Divide the batter evenly among the muffin cups. Bake until the tops are golden and a toothpick inserted in the centers comes out clean, 22 to 25 minutes. Cool on a wire rack before removing from the pan.

MAKES 12 MEDIUM MUFFINS

Devil's Food
Chocolate Chip Muffins

SOME PEOPLE PREFER CAKELIKE MUFFINS. This double-chocolate version is a cross between a cupcake and a muffin, and an excellent one at that. It makes a delicious snack—a sort of cookie substitute—with a glass of milk.

2 cups unbleached all-purpose flour	⅓ cup vegetable oil
⅔ cup unsweetened cocoa powder	2 large eggs
½ cup sugar	1 teaspoon vanilla extract
2 teaspoons baking soda, sieved	1 cup semisweet chocolate chips,
½ teaspoon salt	preferably mini-chips
1⅓ cups milk	

1. Preheat the oven to 400 degrees F. Lightly butter 12 muffin cups or coat with nonstick cooking spray.

2. In a large bowl, combine the flour, cocoa powder, sugar, baking soda and salt; stir to blend.

3. In a separate bowl, whisk together the milk, oil, eggs and vanilla until smooth. Add the liquid ingredients and ½ cup of the chocolate chips to the dry ingredients and fold just until evenly moistened. Do not overmix.

4. Divide the batter evenly among the muffin cups. Sprinkle the muffins evenly with the remaining chocolate chips.

5. Bake until a toothpick inserted in the centers comes out clean, 20 to 22 minutes. Cool on a wire rack before removing from the pan.

MAKES 12
MEDIUM MUFFINS

Espresso Chip Muffins

WHEN I DRINK A CUP OF ESPRESSO, I like it rich, creamy and freshly brewed. I never drink instant espresso because once it is diluted with water, the powder loses its flavor. But when the espresso coffee powder is stirred directly into muffin batter, it adds just the right coffee kick. Give yourself a double treat by enjoying one of these muffins midmorning with a cup of steaming cappuccino.

2 cups unbleached all-purpose flour
¼ cup instant espresso coffee powder
1 tablespoon baking powder
1 teaspoon ground cinnamon
1 teaspoon salt
1 cup milk
¾ cup packed light brown sugar
½ cup (1 stick) unsalted butter, melted

2 large eggs
1 teaspoon vanilla extract
½ cup semisweet
   chocolate chips

1. Preheat the oven to 400 degrees F. Lightly butter 12 muffin cups or coat with nonstick cooking spray.

2. Combine the flour, espresso coffee powder, baking powder, cinnamon and salt in a large bowl; stir to blend. In a separate bowl, whisk together the milk, brown sugar, melted butter, eggs and vanilla until smooth. Add the liquid ingredients to the dry; fold just until the dry ingredients are evenly moistened. Do not overmix.

3. Divide the batter evenly among the muffin cups. Sprinkle a few chocolate chips on top of each muffin. Bake until the edges begin to pull away from the sides and a toothpick inserted in the centers comes out clean, 20 to 22 minutes.

4. Cool on a wire rack before removing from the pan.

MAKES 12 MEDIUM MUFFINS

Favorite Steiger Haus Carrot & Apple Muffins

F LAKED COCONUT AND GRATED CARROT AND APPLE give this muffin great taste and texture. Finely chop chunks of peeled carrot and apple separately in the food processor, using the steel blade. Made with locally grown Oregon hazelnuts, this luscious muffin is a favorite at the Steiger Haus, a lovely bed-and-breakfast in McMinnville, Oregon.

Topping (optional)

2 tablespoons sugar

2 teaspoons ground cinnamon

Batter

2 cups unbleached all-purpose flour

1¼ cups sugar

2 teaspoons baking soda, sieved

2 teaspoons ground cinnamon

½ teaspoon salt

2 cups peeled, grated carrot
(about 4 medium carrots)

1 cup peeled, cored, grated apple
(1 large apple), plus slices for
optional topping

½ cup finely chopped hazelnuts (filberts)

½ cup dried currants or raisins

½ cup flaked sweetened coconut

1 cup vegetable oil

3 large eggs

2 teaspoons vanilla extract

1. **To make the Topping**, if using: In a small bowl, combine the sugar and the cinnamon; set aside.

2. Preheat the oven to 400 degrees F. Lightly butter 12 muffin cups or coat with nonstick cooking spray.

3. **To make the Batter**: Combine the flour, sugar, baking soda, cinnamon and salt in a large bowl. Stir in the carrots, apple, hazelnuts, currants or raisins and coconut.

4. In a separate bowl, whisk together the oil, eggs and vanilla. Add to the dry ingredients all at once and fold just until evenly moistened. Do not overmix.

5. Divide the batter evenly among the muffin cups. Top each muffin with an apple slice, if using, and sprinkle with a little of the optional cinnamon-sugar topping. Bake until the tops are golden and a toothpick inserted in the centers comes out clean, 20 to 25 minutes.

6. Cool on a wire rack before removing from the pan.

MAKES 12 LARGE MUFFINS

Fabulous Banana Muffins

I LOVE THE INTENSE BANANA FLAVOR of these muffins. The texture is just right too: moist and dense—like a banana. These are great warm from the oven or split and reheated in a toaster oven. The recipe comes from friend and cookbook author Michele Scicolone.

2   cups unbleached all-purpose flour
2   teaspoons baking powder
1   teaspoon baking soda, sieved
1   teaspoon salt
½   cup chopped walnuts (optional)

1½   cups mashed ripe banana
       (about 3½ bananas)
⅔   cup packed light brown sugar
⅓   cup (5⅓ tablespoons) unsalted
       butter, melted
1   large egg
1   teaspoon vanilla extract

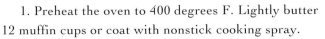

1. Preheat the oven to 400 degrees F. Lightly butter 12 muffin cups or coat with nonstick cooking spray.

2. In a large bowl, combine the flour, baking powder, baking soda and salt; stir until well blended. Stir in the walnuts, if using.

3. In a separate bowl, whisk together the mashed banana, brown sugar, melted butter, egg and vanilla until smooth. Add to the dry ingredients all at once and fold just until evenly moistened. Do not overmix.

4. Divide the batter evenly among the muffin cups. Bake until the tops are golden and a toothpick inserted in the centers comes out clean, 20 to 25 minutes.

5. Cool on a wire rack before removing from the pan.

MAKES 12 MEDIUM MUFFINS

Fig-Nana & Nut Muffins

F IGS AND BANANAS ARE TWO OF MY FAVORITE FOODS, so I decided to combine them in a muffin. Using kitchen scissors whose blades have been rubbed with a little vegetable oil makes it easier to snip the figs into small pieces.

2 cups unbleached all-purpose flour	1½ cups mashed ripe banana
2 teaspoons baking powder	(about 3½ bananas)
1 teaspoon baking soda, sieved	⅔ cup packed light brown sugar
1 teaspoon salt	½ cup (1 stick) unsalted butter, melted
½ cup minced dried (moist-pack)	1 large egg
Calimyrna figs	1 teaspoon vanilla extract
	½ cup coarsely chopped walnuts

1. Preheat the oven to 400 degrees F. Lightly butter 12 muffin cups or coat with nonstick cooking spray.

2. Combine the flour, baking powder, baking soda and salt in a large bowl; stir to blend. Stir in the figs.

3. In a separate bowl, whisk together the mashed banana, brown sugar, melted butter, egg and vanilla until smooth. Add to the dry ingredients all at once and fold just until evenly moistened. Do not overmix.

4. Divide the batter evenly among the muffin cups. Sprinkle the tops evenly with the chopped walnuts. Bake until the tops are golden and a toothpick inserted in the centers comes out clean, 20 to 22 minutes.

5. Cool on a wire rack before removing from the pan.

MAKES 12 LARGE MUFFINS

Ginger Molasses Muffins

D ARK AND MOIST WITH MOLASSES and spicy with ginger, these muffins are for ginger-bread fans. If you want an extra jolt of ginger, add 2 tablespoons finely chopped crystallized ginger to the batter just before baking.

2½   cups unbleached all-purpose flour
½   cup packed light brown sugar
1   tablespoon ground ginger
2   teaspoons baking powder
1   teaspoon baking soda, sieved

½   teaspoon ground cloves
1   cup buttermilk
½   cup unsulphured dark molasses
¼   cup vegetable oil
1   large egg

1. Preheat the oven to 400 degrees F. Lightly butter 12 muffin cups or coat with nonstick cooking spray.

2. Combine the flour, brown sugar, ginger, baking powder, baking soda and cloves in a large bowl; stir until well blended.

3. In a separate bowl, whisk together the buttermilk, molasses, oil and egg. Add to the dry ingredients all at once and fold just until evenly moistened. Do not overmix.

4. Divide the batter evenly among the muffin cups. Bake until the edges begin to pull away from the sides and a toothpick inserted in the centers comes out clean, 20 to 22 minutes.

5. Cool on a wire rack before removing from the pan.

MAKES 12 MEDIUM MUFFINS

Honey Muffins

THESE MUFFINS HAVE SLIGHTLY CRUNCHY TOPS and light, spongy bottoms. Honey gives them a slightly marbled look, contributing not only sweetness but also extra flavor. These are especially nice as a snack with a cup of herb tea.

2	cups unbleached all-purpose flour	½	cup honey
¼	cup sugar	½	cup milk
2	teaspoons baking powder	⅓	cup (5⅓ tablespoons) unsalted
1	teaspoon baking soda, sieved		butter, melted
½	teaspoon salt	1	large egg
¼	teaspoon freshly grated nutmeg		

1. Preheat the oven to 400 degrees F. Lightly butter 12 muffin cups or coat with nonstick cooking spray.

2. Combine the flour, sugar, baking powder, baking soda, salt and nutmeg in a large bowl; stir until well blended. In a separate bowl, whisk together the honey, milk, melted butter and

egg until smooth. Add to the dry ingredients all at once and fold just until evenly moistened. Do not overmix.

3. Divide the batter evenly among the muffin cups. Bake until the tops are golden and a toothpick inserted in the centers comes out clean, about 20 minutes. Cool on a wire rack before removing from the pan.

MAKES 12 MEDIUM MUFFINS

Indian Pudding Muffins

THE COMBINATION OF CRUNCHY CORNMEAL and rich molasses in these muffins is reminiscent of the flavors of that popular New England dessert, Indian pudding. The muffins are delicious as a snack with a mug of hot spiced cider.

1½	cups unbleached all-purpose flour	½	cup packed dark brown sugar
1	cup yellow cornmeal	1	cup buttermilk
1	tablespoon baking powder	½	cup (1 stick) unsalted butter, melted
1	teaspoon baking soda, sieved	½	cup unsulphured dark molasses
½	teaspoon salt	2	large eggs

1. Preheat the oven to 400 degrees F. Lightly butter 12 muffin cups or coat with nonstick cooking spray.

2. Combine the flour, cornmeal, baking powder, baking soda and salt in a large bowl; stir until thoroughly blended. Add the brown sugar and stir until blended.

3. In a separate bowl, whisk together the buttermilk, melted butter, molasses and eggs until blended. Add to the dry ingredients all at once and fold just until evenly moistened. Do not overmix.

4. Divide the batter evenly among the muffin cups. Bake until the edges begin to pull away from the sides of the pan and a toothpick inserted in the centers comes out clean, 20 to 22 minutes.

5. Cool on a wire rack before removing from the pan.

MAKES 12 MEDIUM MUFFINS

J

Jammies

THE SOUR CREAM IN THESE MUFFINS works as both the liquid and the fat and is the secret to the especially tender consistency. The muffins are topped with a dollop of jam just before they are popped into the oven. This idea comes from friend, collaborator and muffin maker extraordinaire Susan Westmoreland. Susan suggests using a different flavor of jam for each muffin, giving a jeweled look to the batch.

2½	cups unbleached all-purpose flour	2	large eggs
½	cup sugar	1	teaspoon vanilla extract
2	teaspoons baking powder	12	teaspoons strawberry, raspberry,
1	teaspoon baking soda, sieved		apricot or other favorite jam or
½	teaspoon salt		preserves
1	container (16 ounces) sour cream		

1. Preheat the oven to 400 degrees F. Lightly butter 12 muffin cups or coat with nonstick cooking spray.

2. Combine the flour, sugar, baking powder, baking soda and salt in a large bowl; stir to blend well. In a separate bowl, whisk together the sour cream, eggs and vanilla until smooth. Add to the dry ingredients all at once and fold just until evenly moistened. Do not overmix.

3. Divide the batter evenly among the muffin cups. Make a small hollow in the batter with the tip of a spoon and spoon 1 teaspoon jam into each hollow.

4. Bake until the tops are golden and the edges pull away from the sides of the cups, 20 to 22 minutes. Cool on a wire rack before removing from the pan.

MAKES 12 MEDIUM MUFFINS

Jalapeño-Cheddar Corn Muffins

I LIKE TO SERVE THESE ZIPPY MUFFINS WITH CHILI. They also make a savory snack, especially when something sweet just isn't right.

½ cup (1 stick) unsalted butter
½ cup chopped onion
1 tablespoon seeded, finely chopped fresh jalapeño pepper
1¾ cups unbleached all-purpose flour
1 cup yellow cornmeal
2 teaspoons baking powder
½ teaspoon baking soda, sieved

½ teaspoon salt
1 cup canned creamed corn (from one 14-ounce can)
1 cup buttermilk
1 large egg
Dash of Tabasco, or more to taste
1½ cups shredded sharp Cheddar cheese

46

1. Preheat the oven to 400 degrees F. Lightly butter 12 muffin cups or coat with nonstick cooking spray.

2. Melt the butter in a large skillet; add the onion and sauté until golden, about 8 minutes. Remove from the heat. Add the jalapeño pepper.

3. Combine the flour, cornmeal, baking powder, baking soda and salt in a large bowl; stir until well blended. In a separate bowl, whisk together the corn, buttermilk, egg, Tabasco and the cooked-onion mixture until blended. Add to the dry ingredients, along with 1 cup of the cheese. Fold until evenly moistened. Do not overmix.

4. Divide the batter evenly among the muffin cups. Sprinkle the tops with the remaining ½ cup cheese, dividing evenly.

5. Bake until the tops are golden and a toothpick inserted in the centers comes out clean, 20 to 22 minutes. Cool on a wire rack before removing from the pan.

MAKES 12 MEDIUM MUFFINS

Knock-Out Muffins

(Banana-Pecan Chocolate Chip Muffins)

WHEN IT COMES TO BAKING, I find anything made with banana especially seductive. But this combination of banana, chocolate and pecan is a real "knock-out."

2 cups unbleached all-purpose flour	1 teaspoon salt
2 teaspoons baking powder	½ cup semisweet chocolate chips
1 teaspoon baking soda, sieved	1½ cups mashed ripe banana (about 3½ bananas)
1 teaspoon ground cinnamon	⅔ cup packed light brown sugar
	⅓ cup (5⅓ tablespoons) unsalted butter, melted
	1 large egg
	1 teaspoon vanilla extract
	½ cup coarsely chopped pecans

1. Preheat the oven to 400 degrees F. Lightly butter 12 muffin cups or coat with nonstick cooking spray.

2. Combine the flour, baking powder, baking soda, cinnamon and salt in a large bowl; stir to blend. Stir in the chocolate chips.

3. In a separate bowl, whisk together the mashed banana, brown sugar, melted butter, egg and vanilla until well blended. Add to the dry ingredients all at once and fold until evenly moistened. Do not overmix.

4. Divide the batter evenly among the muffin cups. Sprinkle the tops evenly with the chopped pecans. Bake until the tops are golden and a toothpick inserted in the centers comes out clean, about 20 minutes.

5. Cool on a wire rack before removing from the pan.

MAKES 12 MEDIUM MUFFINS

Lemon-Drizzled Lemon Muffins

Grated lemon zest adds a soft, subtle flavor to the cake portion of these muffins, while the fresh lemon juice and confectioners' sugar glaze give a sparkle to every bite. Made in miniature muffin cups, they look especially dainty.

Batter

2	cups unbleached all-purpose flour
½	cup sugar
2	teaspoons baking powder
½	teaspoon baking soda, sieved
½	teaspoon salt
2	teaspoons grated lemon zest
1	cup plain low-fat yogurt
¼	cup vegetable oil
1	large egg
1	teaspoon vanilla extract

Lemon Drizzle

½	cup confectioners' sugar
1	tablespoon fresh lemon juice

Muffins A *to* Z

1. Preheat the oven to 400 degrees F. Lightly butter 12 muffin cups or 24 small muffin cups or coat with non-stick cooking spray.

2. **To make the Batter**: Combine the flour, sugar, baking powder, baking soda, salt and lemon zest in a large bowl; stir until well blended. In a separate bowl, whisk together the yogurt, oil, egg and vanilla until smooth. Add to the dry ingredients all at once and fold just until evenly moistened. Do not overmix.

3. Divide the batter among the muffin cups. Bake until the tops are golden and a toothpick inserted in the centers comes out clean, about 20 minutes (15 minutes for miniature muffins). Cool slightly.

4. **To make the Lemon Drizzle**: Stir the confectioners' sugar and lemon juice together until smooth. Using a teaspoon, drizzle the mixture over the tops of the muffins while they are still warm. Let the muffins cool completely and the drizzle set before removing from the pan.

MAKES 12 MEDIUM OR 24 SMALL MUFFINS

Marmalade Muffins

THE CHARACTERISTICALLY BITTERSWEET TASTE of the marmalade in the center is a pleasant counterpoint to the sweetness of this cakey muffin. The recipe comes from Doris Steiger of the Steiger Haus, a bed-and-breakfast in McMinnville, Oregon.

2 cups all-purpose unbleached flour	1 teaspoon vanilla extract
⅔ cup sugar	½ teaspoon almond extract
2 teaspoons baking powder	½ cup (approximately) orange marmalade
½ teaspoon salt	
1 cup milk	½ cup sliced natural (unblanched) almonds
½ cup (1 stick) unsalted butter, melted	
1 large egg	Confectioners' sugar

1. Preheat the oven to 400 degrees F. Lightly butter 12 muffin cups or coat with nonstick cooking spray.

2. Combine the flour, sugar, baking powder and salt in a large bowl; stir to blend.

3. In a separate bowl, whisk together the milk, melted butter, egg and vanilla and almond extracts until blended. Add to the dry ingredients all at once and fold together just until evenly moistened. Do not overmix.

4. Fill the muffin cups almost half full with the batter. Place a rounded teaspoonful of marmalade on top of the batter in the center of each cup. Top with the remaining batter, dividing evenly. Sprinkle the tops with the almonds.

5. Bake until the tops are golden and the edges begin to pull away from the sides, about 20 minutes.

6. Cool on a wire rack before removing from the pan. Sift a little confectioners' sugar on top of each muffin.

MAKES 12 MEDIUM MUFFINS

Molasses Bran Muffins

A WHOLE CUP OF MOLASSES gives these muffins a deep, dark flavor that I love. The bran adds crunch and a nutty taste. I like these made with plump, organically grown raisins, but any chopped dried fruit (apricots, peaches, prunes) will work.

1	cup bran cereal (All-Bran or 100% Bran)	1	tablespoon baking powder
1½	cups milk	1	teaspoon baking soda, sieved
1	cup unsulphured dark molasses	½	teaspoon salt
½	cup vegetable oil	½	cup raisins or any other minced dried fruit (apricots, pears, peaches, prunes or figs)
1	large egg		
2	cups unbleached all-purpose flour		

1. Preheat the oven to 400 degrees F. Lightly butter 12 muffin cups or coat with nonstick cooking spray.

2. Combine the bran cereal and milk in a medium bowl and let stand for 5 minutes. Add the molasses, oil and egg; stir until well blended.

3. In a large bowl, combine the flour, baking powder, baking soda and salt; stir to blend well. Add the liquid ingredients and the dried fruit and fold just until blended. Do not over-mix.

4. Divide the batter evenly among the muffin cups. Bake until the edges begin to pull away from the sides and a toothpick inserted in the centers comes out clean, 20 to 22 minutes.

5. Cool on a wire rack before removing from the pan.

MAKES 12 MEDIUM MUFFINS

Nantucket Morning Glory Muffins

A LONG TIME AGO, on the island of Nantucket, I remember nibbling a muffin like this at a popular breakfast spot called The Morning Glory Cafe. These moist muffins are packed full of shredded carrot, zucchini, raisins and walnuts—and memories.

1 cup whole wheat flour
1 cup unbleached all-purpose flour
1 tablespoon baking powder
1 teaspoon ground cinnamon
½ teaspoon baking soda, sieved
½ teaspoon salt
⅔ cup packed light brown sugar
1 cup coarsely shredded zucchini
  (about 2 small zucchini, trimmed),
  lightly packed

½ cup coarsely shredded carrot
  (1 medium carrot), lightly packed
¾ cup golden raisins
1 cup chopped walnuts
1 cup buttermilk
⅓ cup vegetable oil
1 large egg

1. Preheat the oven to 400 degrees F. Lightly butter 12 muffin cups or coat with nonstick cooking spray.

2. Combine the flours, baking powder, cinnamon, baking soda and salt in a large bowl; stir until thoroughly blended. Add the brown sugar and stir to blend. Stir in the zucchini, carrot, raisins and ½ cup of the walnuts.

3. In a separate bowl, whisk together the buttermilk, oil and egg until blended. Add to the dry ingredients all at once and fold just until evenly moistened. Do not overmix.

4. Divide the batter evenly among the muffin cups. Sprinkle the tops with the remaining ½ cup walnuts, dividing evenly. Bake until the tops are golden and a toothpick inserted in the centers comes out clean, about 25 minutes.

5. Cool on a wire rack before removing from the pan.

MAKES 12 LARGE MUFFINS

Oatmeal & Cranberry Muffins

S OAKING THE OATS IN MILK before adding them to the batter gives these tender muffins an especially moist taste and texture. They are good for breakfast.

1½ cups milk	2 teaspoons baking powder
1⅓ cups old-fashioned rolled oats, plus more for optional topping	1 teaspoon baking soda, sieved
⅓ cup (5⅓ tablespoons) unsalted butter, cut into pieces	½ teaspoon salt
	2 large eggs
1⅓ cups unbleached all-purpose flour	1½ cups fresh or frozen cranberries
¾ cup packed light brown sugar	½ cup raisins

1. In a small saucepan, combine the milk and the oats; bring to a boil over medium heat. Remove from the heat and stir in the butter. Cool slightly.

2. Preheat the oven to 425 degrees F. Lightly butter 12 muffin cups or coat with nonstick cooking spray.

3. Combine the flour, brown sugar, baking powder, baking soda and salt in a large bowl; stir until blended.

4. Add the eggs to the oat mixture and stir until well blended. Add the oat mixture to the dry ingredients, along with cranberries and raisins, and fold just until evenly moistened. Do not overmix.

5. Divide the batter evenly among the muffin cups; sprinkle each muffin with oats, if desired. Bake until a toothpick inserted in the centers comes out clean, 20 to 22 minutes. Cool on a wire rack before removing from the pan.

MAKES 12 MEDIUM MUFFINS

Peanut Peanut-Butter Muffins

DOUBLE PEANUT FLAVOR makes these muffins twice as good. Densely peanutty, these muffins are popular with peanut butter lovers of all ages.

½   cup smooth peanut butter
¾   cup packed light brown sugar
2   large eggs
1   teaspoon vanilla extract
2½ cups unbleached all-purpose flour

1½ teaspoons baking soda, sieved
½   teaspoon salt
1½ cups buttermilk
½   cup chopped dry-roasted
     unsalted peanuts

1. Preheat the oven to 400 degrees F. Lightly butter 12 muffin cups or coat with nonstick cooking spray.

2. With a mixer, beat the peanut butter and brown sugar together in a large bowl until well blended. Beat in the eggs, one at a time, beating well after each addition. Beat in the vanilla.

3. In a large bowl, combine the flour, baking soda and salt; stir until blended. Fold the dry ingredients and the buttermilk alternately into the peanut butter mixture, beginning and ending with the dry ingredients. Do not overmix.

4. Divide the batter evenly among the muffin cups. Sprinkle each muffin with 1 heaping teaspoon of the chopped peanuts.

5. Bake until a toothpick inserted in the centers comes out clean, 20 to 22 minutes. Cool on a wire rack before removing from the pan.

MAKES 12 MEDIUM MUFFINS

Pumpkin Praline Muffins

PUMPKIN, BROWN SUGAR AND PECANS have a natural affinity for one another. These slightly sweet, moist, cakey muffins have an almost candylike praline topping. They make a great treat for breakfast and are especially good served on Thanksgiving morning. The leftover pumpkin can be frozen for later use.

Topping

3 tablespoons unsalted butter, softened
⅓ cup unbleached all-purpose flour
⅓ cup packed light brown sugar
1 cup coarsely chopped or broken
  pecans

1 teaspoon ground cinnamon
½ teaspoon ground ginger
½ teaspoon salt
¼ teaspoon ground cloves
½ cup packed light brown sugar
1 cup mashed pumpkin (from one
  16-ounce solid-pack can)

Batter

2 cups unbleached all-purpose flour
2 teaspoons baking powder
1 teaspoon baking soda, sieved

½ cup unsulphured dark molasses
1 large egg
1 teaspoon vanilla extract

1. Preheat the oven to 400 degrees F. Lightly butter 12 muffin cups or coat with nonstick cooking spray.

2. **To make the Topping:** Cream the butter, flour and brown sugar together in a small bowl until smooth. Blend in the pecans; set aside.

3. **To make the Batter:** Combine the flour, baking powder, baking soda, cinnamon, ginger, salt and cloves in a large bowl; stir until well blended. Add the brown sugar and stir to blend.

4. In a separate bowl, whisk together the pumpkin, molasses, egg and vanilla until smooth. Add to the dry ingredients all at once and fold just until evenly moistened. Do not overmix.

5. Divide the batter evenly among the muffin cups. Press 1 tablespoonful of the reserved praline topping onto the tops of each of the muffins. Bake until the edges begin to pull away from the sides and a toothpick inserted in the centers comes out clean, 20 to 22 minutes. Cool on a wire rack before removing from the pan.

MAKES 12 MEDIUM MUFFINS

Prune & Oat Muffins with Orange

PRUNE AND ORANGE is one of my favorite flavor combinations. These muffins are pleasantly crunchy with uncooked oatmeal.

1 **cup unbleached all-purpose flour**	½ **teaspoon salt**
½ **cup whole wheat flour**	1 **cup milk**
1 **cup quick (not instant) oatmeal or**	½ **cup (1 stick) unsalted butter, melted**
old-fashioned rolled oats	1 **large egg**
½ **cup packed light brown sugar**	1 **cup snipped (moist-pack)**
1 **tablespoon baking powder**	**pitted prunes**
1 **tablespoon grated orange zest**	

1. Preheat the oven to 400 degrees F. Lightly butter 12 muffin cups or coat with nonstick cooking spray.

2. Combine the flours, oatmeal or oats, brown sugar, baking powder, orange zest and salt in a large bowl. In a separate bowl, whisk together the milk, melted butter and egg until blended. Add the liquid ingredients to the dry all at once, along with the prunes, and fold just until evenly moistened. Do not overmix.

3. Divide the batter evenly among the muffin cups. Bake until the tops are golden and a toothpick inserted in the centers comes out clean, 20 to 22 minutes. Cool on a wire rack before removing from the pan.

MAKES 12 MEDIUM MUFFINS

Quickie-Mix Muffins

KEEP THIS DRY MIX ON HAND, and your muffins will take just minutes. Buttermilk, yogurt and sour cream all yield tender muffins and are recommended for this mix. If you do not have any, place 1 tablespoon vinegar or lemon juice in the bottom of a 2-cup measure and fill with the amount of milk required, then proceed with the recipe.

Quickie Mix

10 cups unbleached all-purpose flour

1 cup sugar

3 tablespoons baking powder

4 teaspoons baking soda, sieved

2 teaspoons salt

For Each Muffin Batch

1½ cups buttermilk, yogurt or sour cream

¼ cup vegetable oil

2 large eggs

2⅔ cups Quickie Mix

1. **To make the Quickie Mix**: Stir the flour, sugar, baking powder, baking soda and salt until well blended in a large airtight container or combine in a large bowl and transfer to a resealable plastic bag. Store at room temperature for up to 1 month. (Makes enough for 4 dozen muffins.)

2. **To make the Muffins**: Preheat the oven to 400 degrees F. Lightly butter 12 muffin cups or coat with nonstick cooking spray.

3. Whisk the buttermilk, yogurt or sour cream with the oil and eggs in a medium bowl until well blended.

4. Place 2⅔ cups of the Quickie Mix in a separate large bowl. Add the liquid ingredients all at once and fold just until evenly moistened. Do not overmix.

5. Divide the batter evenly among the muffin cups. Bake until a toothpick inserted in the centers comes out clean, 20 to 22 minutes. Cool on a wire rack before removing from the pan.

MAKES 12 MEDIUM MUFFINS

Variations

Chocolate Chip-Yogurt Muffins: Add ¼ cup additional sugar to the 2⅔ cups of the Quickie Mix. Fold ¾ cup miniature semisweet chocolate chips into the mix, along with the liquid ingredients.

Date-Nut & Coffee Muffins: Substitute fresh-brewed coffee for the buttermilk, yogurt or sour cream. Fold 1 cup chopped dates, ¼ cup light brown sugar and ½ cup chopped walnuts or pecans into the 2⅔ cups of the Quickie Mix, along with the coffee.

Banana Muffins: Substitute 2 or 3 mashed bananas, plus enough milk to equal 1½ cups, for the buttermilk, yogurt or sour cream and add to the 2⅔ cups of the Quickie Mix.

Blueberry Muffins: Add ¼ cup additional sugar to the 2⅔ cups of the Quickie Mix. Pick over, rinse and dry 1½ to 2 cups blueberries, toss them with 1 tablespoon flour and add them to the mix along with the liquid ingredients. Frozen berries may be substituted; it is not necessary to thaw them. Sprinkle the muffins with additional sugar before baking, if desired.

Raisin Bran Muffins

THESE CLASSIC BRAN MUFFINS are especially low in fat, containing only about 5 grams each, because much of the vegetable oil has been replaced with low-fat or nonfat yogurt. They are dark and moist, as good bran muffins should be.

1	cup bran cereal (All-Bran or 100% Bran)	1	teaspoon ground cinnamon
1	cup low-fat or nonfat plain yogurt	1	cup raisins
1	cup unbleached all-purpose flour	½	cup unsulphured dark molasses
2	teaspoons baking powder	¼	cup vegetable oil
1	teaspoon baking soda, sieved	1	large egg
		1	teaspoon vanilla extract

1. Preheat the oven to 400 degrees F. Lightly butter 12 muffin cups or coat with nonstick cooking spray.

2. Combine the bran cereal and yogurt in a small bowl; set aside.

3. Combine the flour, baking powder, baking soda and cinnamon in a large bowl; stir to blend. Stir in the raisins.

4. In a separate bowl, whisk together the molasses, oil, egg and vanilla. Add the bran mixture and the molasses mixture to the dry ingredients all at once and fold just until evenly moistened. Do not overmix.

5. Divide the batter equally among the muffin cups. Bake until a toothpick inserted in the centers comes out clean, 20 to 22 minutes. Cool on a wire rack before removing from the pan.

MAKES 12 MEDIUM MUFFINS

Ricotta-Lemon Muffins

RICOTTA MAKES ESPECIALLY LIGHT, tender muffins. Enjoy these when they are fresh and warm; they do not age well.

2½ cups unbleached all-purpose flour

⅓ cup sugar

2 teaspoons baking powder

1 teaspoon baking soda, sieved

½ teaspoon salt

Pinch of ground cinnamon

1 cup whole-milk ricotta cheese

¾ cup milk

⅓ cup (5⅓ tablespoons) unsalted butter, melted

2 large eggs

1 teaspoon grated lemon zest

1 teaspoon vanilla extract

1. Preheat the oven to 400 degrees F. Lightly butter 12 muffin cups or coat with nonstick cooking spray.

2. Combine the flour, sugar, baking powder, baking soda, salt and cinnamon in a large bowl; stir until blended.

3. In a separate bowl, whisk together the ricotta, milk, melted butter, eggs, lemon zest and vanilla until well blended. Add to the dry ingredients all at once and stir just until evenly moistened. Do not overmix.

4. Divide the batter evenly among the muffin cups. Bake until a toothpick inserted in the centers comes out clean, 20 to 22 minutes. Cool on a wire rack before removing from the pan.

MAKES 12 LARGE MUFFINS

Strawberry Muffins

T HESE MUFFINS ARE PARTICULARLY GOOD with fresh strawberries, but this recipe
can also be made with blueberries or peaches.

2½ cups unbleached all-purpose flour

½ cup sugar, plus more for optional topping

2 teaspoons baking powder

1 teaspoon baking soda, sieved

½ teaspoon salt

1¼ cups buttermilk

⅓ cup (5⅓ tablespoons) unsalted butter, melted

2 large eggs

1 teaspoon vanilla extract

1¼ cups chopped hulled strawberries (about 1 pint)

1. Preheat the oven to 400 degrees F. Lightly butter 12 muffin cups or coat with nonstick cooking spray.

2. Combine the flour, sugar, baking powder, baking soda and salt in a large bowl; stir until well blended.

3. In a separate bowl, whisk together the buttermilk, melted butter, eggs and vanilla until well blended. Add to the dry ingredients all at once, along with strawberries, and fold just until evenly moistened. Do not overmix.

4. Divide the batter evenly among the muffin cups. Sprinkle each muffin with a little sugar, if desired. Bake until a toothpick inserted in the centers comes out clean, 22 to 25 minutes. Cool on a wire rack before removing from the pan.

MAKES 12 MEDIUM MUFFINS

Savory Scallion Muffins

COOKING THE SCALLIONS IN THE MELTED BUTTER before adding them to the batter gives these muffins a delicate flavor. They are especially nice made as mini-muffins and served with a green salad and a disk of creamy fresh goat cheese.

5 tablespoons unsalted butter	1 teaspoon baking soda, sieved
1 cup chopped scallions (about 1 bunch)	½ teaspoon salt
1½ cups unbleached all-purpose flour	¼ teaspoon ground red pepper (cayenne)
1 cup yellow cornmeal	
1 tablespoon sugar	1⅓ cups buttermilk
2 teaspoons baking powder	2 large eggs

1. Preheat the oven to 400 degrees F. Lightly butter 12 muffin cups or coat with nonstick cooking spray.

2. In a large skillet, melt the butter over medium heat; add the scallions and cook until wilted, about 3 minutes.

3. In a large bowl, combine the flour, cornmeal, sugar, baking powder, baking soda, salt and red pepper; stir until well blended.

4. In a separate bowl, whisk together the buttermilk, eggs and scallion mixture. Add to the dry ingredients and fold just until evenly moistened.

5. Divide the batter evenly among the muffin cups. Bake until a toothpick inserted in the centers comes out clean, 20 to 22 minutes. Cool on a wire rack before removing from the pan.

MAKES 12 MEDIUM MUFFINS

Streusel Coffee Cake Muffins

WHEN I WAS A CHILD, crumb cakes were favorites of mine. But much to my mother's chagrin, I wanted to eat the crumbs off the top and feed the rest to the family pets. When I started baking, learning to make streusel, or crumb topping, was one of my happiest accomplishments.

Topping

3 tablespoons unsalted butter, softened
¼ cup packed light brown sugar
¼ cup quick (not instant) oatmeal or old-fashioned rolled oats
¼ cup unbleached all purpose flour
¼ cup chopped walnuts
½ teaspoon ground cinnamon

Batter

2 cups unbleached all-purpose flour
⅔ cup packed light brown sugar
1 tablespoon baking powder
½ teaspoon baking soda, sieved
1 teaspoon ground cinnamon
1 cup buttermilk
½ cup (1 stick) unsalted butter, melted
1 large egg

1. Preheat the oven to 400 degrees F. Lightly butter 12 muffin cups or coat with nonstick cooking spray.

2. **To make the Topping**: Combine the butter, brown sugar, oatmeal or oats, flour, walnuts and cinnamon in a medium bowl. Stir with a fork or mix with your fingertips until the ingredients are blended and the mixture is crumbly. Set aside.

3. **To make the Batter**: In a large bowl, combine the flour, brown sugar, baking powder, baking soda and cinnamon; stir until well blended. In a separate bowl, whisk together the buttermilk, melted butter and egg. Add to the dry ingredients all at once and fold until evenly moistened. Do not overmix.

4. Divide the batter evenly among the muffin cups. Sprinkle the topping evenly over the tops. Bake until the tops are golden and a toothpick inserted in the centers comes out clean, 20 to 22 minutes.

5. Cool on a wire rack before removing from the pan.

MAKES 12 MEDIUM MUFFINS

Sweet Potato &
Sugared Pecan Muffins

EVER SINCE I DISCOVERED THAT SWEET POTATOES make great muffins, they have become a staple in my pantry bin. These muffins are moist and just sweet enough. Serve them warm. I like them for breakfast. They are good enough to enjoy without butter.

To cook the sweet potatoes for the batter, bake them in a preheated 400-degree oven until soft, about 45 to 55 minutes, or microwave them on high for 10 to 12 minutes, or until tender; remove the skin and mash.

Topping

¼ cup packed dark brown sugar

¼ cup chopped pecans

Batter

2½ cups unbleached all-purpose flour

⅓ cup packed dark brown sugar

2 teaspoons baking powder

1 teaspoon baking soda, sieved

½ teaspoon salt

1 cup mashed cooked sweet potatoes
   (2 medium sweet potatoes)

1⅓ cups buttermilk

¼ cup (½ stick) unsalted butter, melted

2 large eggs

1. Preheat the oven to 400 degrees F. Lightly butter 12 muffin cups or coat with nonstick cooking spray.

2. **To make the Topping**: Stir the brown sugar and pecans together in a small bowl until blended. Set aside.

3. **To make the Batter**: In a large bowl, combine the flour, brown sugar, baking powder, baking soda and salt; stir until well blended. In a small bowl, whisk together the sweet potatoes, buttermilk, melted butter and eggs. Add to the dry ingredients all at once and fold just until evenly moistened. Do not overmix.

4. Divide the batter evenly among the muffin cups. Sprinkle each muffin with 1 heaping teaspoon of the topping. Bake until a toothpick inserted in the centers comes out clean, 20 to 22 minutes. Cool on a wire rack before removing from the pan.

MAKES 12 MEDIUM MUFFINS

Toasted Almond & Apricot Muffins

O F THE ENORMOUS VARIETY OF DRIED FRUITS now available, I still like apricots—a childhood favorite—the best. And apricots and almonds are a classic combination that is hard to beat.

2 cups unbleached all-purpose flour	1 large egg
⅔ cup packed light brown sugar	½ teaspoon vanilla extract
1 tablespoon baking powder	¼ teaspoon almond extract
½ teaspoon baking soda, sieved	½ cup diced dried apricots
½ teaspoon salt	⅓ cup sliced natural (unblanched)
1 cup buttermilk	almonds
½ cup (1 stick) unsalted butter, melted	

1. Preheat the oven to 400 degrees F. Lightly butter 12 muffin cups or coat with nonstick cooking spray.

2. Combine the flour, brown sugar, baking powder, baking soda and salt in a large bowl; stir until well blended.

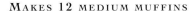

3. In a separate bowl, whisk together the buttermilk, melted butter, egg and vanilla and almond extracts. Stir the apricots into the dry ingredients. Add the liquid ingredients all at once and fold until evenly moistened. Do not overmix.

4. Divide the batter evenly among the muffin cups. Sprinkle the almonds evenly on the tops. Bake until the tops are golden and a toothpick inserted in the centers comes out clean, 20 to 22 minutes.

5. Cool on a wire rack before removing from the pan.

MAKES 12 MEDIUM MUFFINS

Upside-Down Muffins

THESE CAKEY MUFFINS WILL TURN OUT OF THE PAN PERFECTLY if they are allowed to cool thoroughly first. Carefully lift them from the muffin cups and place them bottom end up. If any of the muffin remains in the pan, remove with a teaspoon and place on the top of the muffin.

Apple Layer
2   cups diced, peeled, cored baking apples (Golden Delicious, Rome Beauty or Granny Smith, about 2 large)
¼   cup raisins
½   cup packed light brown sugar
1   teaspoon ground cinnamon
2   tablespoons (¼ stick) unsalted butter

Batter
2   cups unbleached all-purpose flour
1   tablespoon baking powder
½   teaspoon baking soda, sieved
½   teaspoon salt
½   cup packed light brown sugar
1   cup buttermilk
½   cup (1 stick) unsalted butter, melted
1   large egg
1   teaspoon vanilla extract

1. Preheat the oven to 400 degrees F. Lightly butter 12 muffin cups or coat with nonstick cooking spray.

2. **To make the Apple Layer**: Combine the apples, raisins, brown sugar and cinnamon in a small bowl; stir until well blended. Melt the butter in a skillet and add the apple mixture. Cook, stirring, over low heat, until the apples are tender, about 5 minutes. Cool.

3. Spoon a single layer of the apple mixture into the muffin cups, dividing evenly.

4. **To make the Batter**: Combine the flour, baking powder, baking soda and salt in a large bowl; stir until well blended. Stir in the brown sugar until blended. In a separate bowl, whisk together the buttermilk, melted butter, egg and vanilla until smooth. Add to the dry ingredients all at once; fold just until evenly moistened. Do not overmix.

5. Divide the batter evenly among the muffin cups. Bake until the tops are golden and a toothpick inserted in the centers comes out clean, 20 to 22 minutes. Cool on a wire rack before removing from the pan.

MAKES 12 MEDIUM MUFFINS

Vagabond Muffins

W HENEVER I GO ON A TRIP — either business or pleasure — I take one of these delectable muffins along. They are so chock-full of good things — apples, raisins, nuts and seeds — that they are nutritious as well as truly satisfying and a vast improvement over airplane food. I freeze them, one or two to a small resealable plastic bag, so they are always packed and ready to go.

½ cup unsalted raw or toasted sunflower seeds, plus 2 tablespoons for optional topping

1 cup whole wheat flour

1 cup unbleached all-purpose flour

1 tablespoon baking powder

½ teaspoon baking soda, sieved

1 teaspoon ground cinnamon

½ teaspoon salt

¼ teaspoon freshly grated nutmeg

⅔ cup packed light brown sugar

1 cup peeled, cored, finely chopped apple (1 large apple)

½ cup raisins

½ cup chopped walnuts

2 tablespoons sesame seeds, preferably with hulls (available in health-food stores)

1 cup buttermilk

½ cup vegetable oil

1 large egg

1. Preheat the oven to 400 degrees F. Lightly butter 12 muffin cups or coat with non-stick cooking spray.

2. If using raw sunflower seeds, toast them in a skillet over low heat, stirring, for about 5 minutes. Set aside.

3. Combine the flours, baking powder, baking soda, cinnamon, salt and nutmeg in a large bowl; stir until well blended. Add the brown sugar and stir to blend. Stir in the apple, raisins, walnuts, sunflower seeds and sesame seeds.

4. In a separate bowl, whisk together the buttermilk, oil and egg. Add to the dry ingredients all at once and fold just until evenly moistened. Do not overmix.

5. Divide the batter evenly among the muffin cups. Sprinkle each muffin with some of the sunflower seeds, if desired. Bake until the tops are lightly browned and a toothpick inserted in the centers comes out clean, about 20 minutes. Cool on a wire rack before removing from the pans.

MAKES 12 LARGE MUFFINS

Wholesome Whole Wheat & Date Muffins

THESE LARGE, TENDER MUFFINS have a great nutty taste and are studded with tiny bits of sweet dates. Sprinkle the tops with chopped walnuts before baking, if you like.

1½ cups whole wheat flour	1 cup chopped dates
1 cup unbleached all-purpose flour	1 cup buttermilk
2 teaspoons baking powder	1 cup vegetable oil
1 teaspoon baking soda, sieved	½ cup packed light brown sugar
1 teaspoon ground cinnamon	1 large egg
¼ teaspoon freshly grated nutmeg	

1. Preheat the oven to 400 degrees F. Lightly butter 12 muffin cups or coat with nonstick cooking spray.

2. In a large bowl, combine the flours, baking powder, baking soda, cinnamon and nutmeg. Stir until thoroughly blended. Stir in the dates.

3. In a separate bowl, whisk together the buttermilk, oil, brown sugar and egg. Add to the

dry ingredients all at once and fold just until evenly moistened. Do not overmix.

4. Divide the batter evenly among the muffin cups. Bake until the edges begin to pull away from the sides and a toothpick inserted in the centers comes out clean, 20 to 22 minutes.

5. Cool on a wire rack before removing from the pan.

MAKES 12 MEDIUM MUFFINS

X

X-tra Muffins
(Cappuccino Chip Muffins)

ONE CAN NEVER BE TOO RICH or too thin—or have enough muffin recipes. Here is an extra. This not-too-sweet muffin has a creamy coffee flavor. Enjoy one with a steaming cup of cappuccino.

2½ cups unbleached all-purpose flour

½ cup sugar

2½ teaspoons baking powder

¼ teaspoon baking soda, sieved

½ teaspoon salt

½ cup semisweet chocolate chips

¾ cup brewed espresso or strong black coffee

½ cup (1 stick) unsalted butter, melted

¼ cup heavy cream

2 large eggs

1 teaspoon vanilla extract

1. Preheat the oven to 400 degrees F. Lightly butter 12 muffin cups or coat with nonstick cooking spray.

2. Combine the flour, sugar, baking powder, baking soda and salt in a large bowl; stir until thoroughly blended. Stir in the chocolate chips.

3. In a separate bowl, whisk together the espresso or coffee, butter, cream, eggs and vanilla. Add to the dry ingredients and fold together until evenly moistened. Do not overmix.

4. Divide the batter evenly among the muffin cups. Bake until the edges begin to pull away from the sides and a toothpick inserted into the centers comes out clean, about 20 minutes. Cool on a wire rack for 5 minutes before removing from the pan.

MAKES 12 MEDIUM MUFFINS

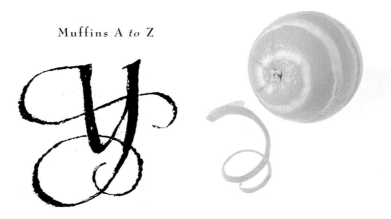

Yogurt-Orange Muffins

NUTMEG AND CLOVE SPICE UP this delicate orange-infused muffin. Muffins made with yogurt are tender and are at their very best when served warm from the oven, either fresh-baked or reheated.

2 cups unbleached all-purpose flour	¼ cup vegetable oil
½ cup sugar	2 large eggs
2 teaspoons baking powder	1 teaspoon vanilla extract
½ teaspoon baking soda, sieved	
½ teaspoon salt	
¼ teaspoon freshly grated nutmeg	
⅛ teaspoon ground cloves	
1 tablespoon finely grated orange zest	
1 cup plain low-fat yogurt	

1. Preheat the oven to 400 degrees F. Lightly butter 12 muffin cups or coat with nonstick cooking spray.

2. In a large bowl, combine the flour, sugar, baking powder, baking soda, salt, nutmeg and cloves; stir until well blended. Stir in the orange zest.

3. In a separate bowl, whisk together the yogurt, oil, eggs and vanilla. Add to the dry ingredients all at once and fold just until evenly moistened. Do not overmix.

4. Divide the batter evenly among the muffin cups. Bake until the tops are lightly browned and a toothpick inserted into the centers comes out clean, about 25 minutes.

MAKES 12 MEDIUM MUFFINS

Zucchini-Romano Muffins

BRIGHTEN YOUR BREAD BASKET with these pretty muffins. The shredded zucchini retains its green color and adds moisture. Pecorino Romano is a sharp, tangy cheese made from sheep's milk. Add more black pepper if you like a lot of spice.

2½ cups unbleached all-purpose flour

½ cup freshly grated Pecorino Romano cheese, plus more for topping

1 tablespoon sugar

2 teaspoons baking powder

1 teaspoon baking soda, sieved

1-2 teaspoons coarsely ground black pepper

¼ teaspoon salt

1 cup milk

1 cup tightly packed coarsely shredded zucchini (about 2 small zucchini, trimmed)

¼ cup olive oil

2 large eggs

1. Preheat the oven to 400 degrees F. Lightly butter 12 muffin cups or coat with nonstick cooking spray.

2. Combine the flour, cheese, sugar, baking powder, baking soda, pepper and salt in a large bowl; stir until blended.

3. In a separate bowl, whisk together the milk, zucchini, oil and eggs. Add to the dry ingredients all at once and fold together just until evenly moistened. Do not overmix.

4. Divide the batter evenly among the muffin cups. Sprinkle each muffin with a little cheese, if desired. Bake until a toothpick inserted in the centers comes out clean, 22 to 25 minutes. Cool on a wire rack before removing from the pan.

MAKES 12 MEDIUM MUFFINS

Index